I0821395

All About Animals
Animal Colors
Maria Koran
EYEDISCOVER

Go to www.eyediscover.com and enter this book's unique code.

BOOK CODE

AVF25438

EYEDISCOVER brings you optic readalongs that support active learning.

Published by AV² by Weigl
350 5th Avenue, 59th Floor New York, NY 10118
Website: www.eyediscover.com

Library of Congress Cataloging-in-Publication Data available on request

ISBN 978-1-7911-0748-2 (hardcover)

Printed in Guangzhou, China
1 2 3 4 5 6 7 8 9 0 23 22 21 20 19

072019
121818

Project Coordinator: John Willis
Designer: Mandy Christiansen and Sushant Deshpande

Weigl acknowledges Alamy, iStock, and Minden Pictures as the primary image suppliers for this title.

EYEDISCOVER provides enriched content, optimized for tablet use, that supplements and complements this book. EYEDISCOVER books strive to create inspired learning and engage young minds in a total learning experience.

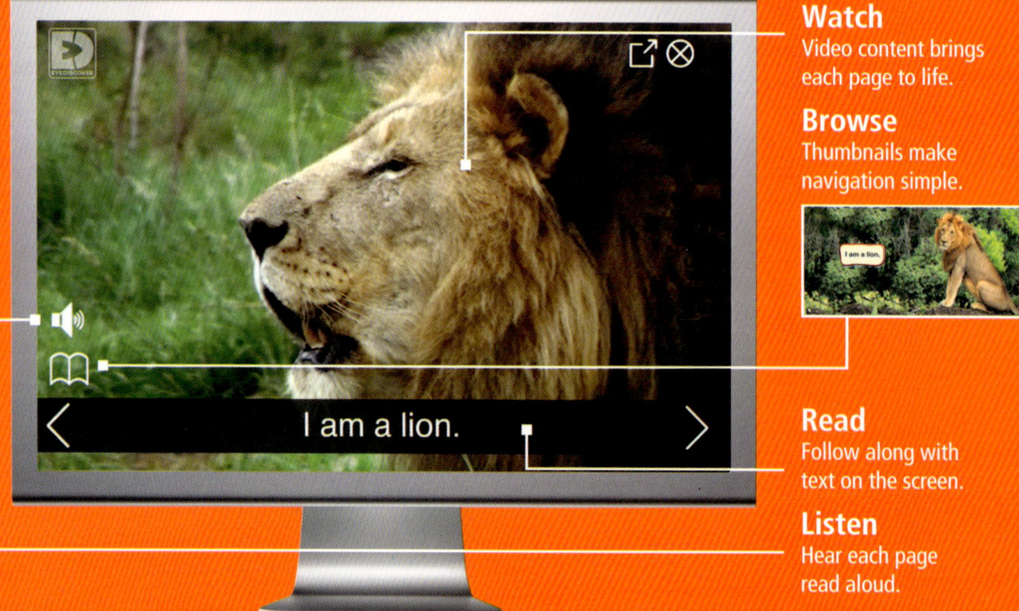

Your EYEDISCOVER Optic Readalongs come alive with...

Audio
Listen to the entire book read aloud.

Video
High resolution videos turn each spread into an optic readalong.

OPTIMIZED FOR

- ✓ TABLETS
- ✓ WHITEBOARDS
- ✓ COMPUTERS
- ✓ AND MUCH MORE!

Animal Colors

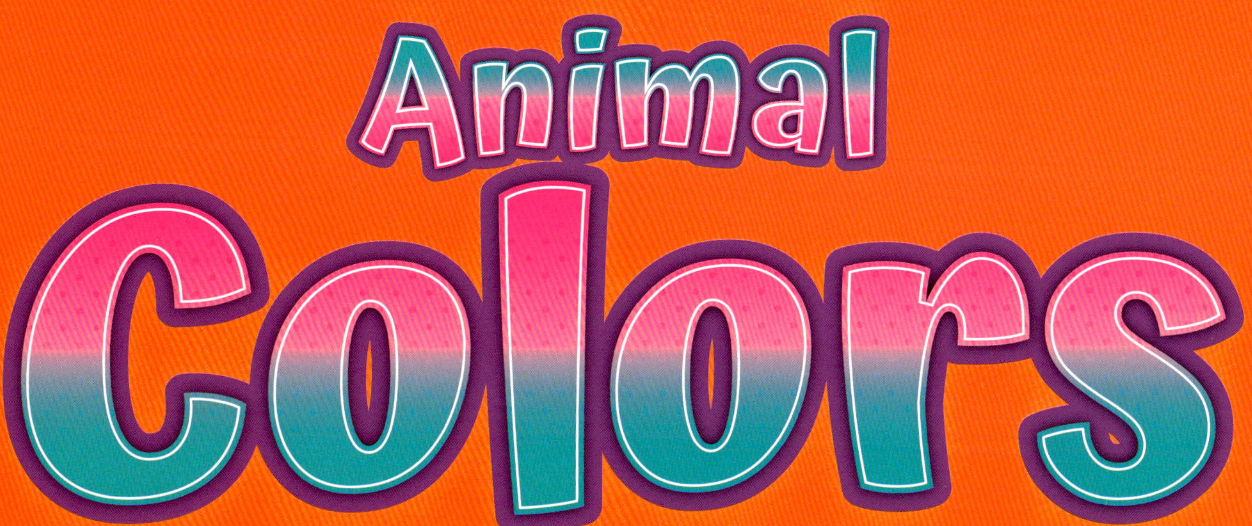

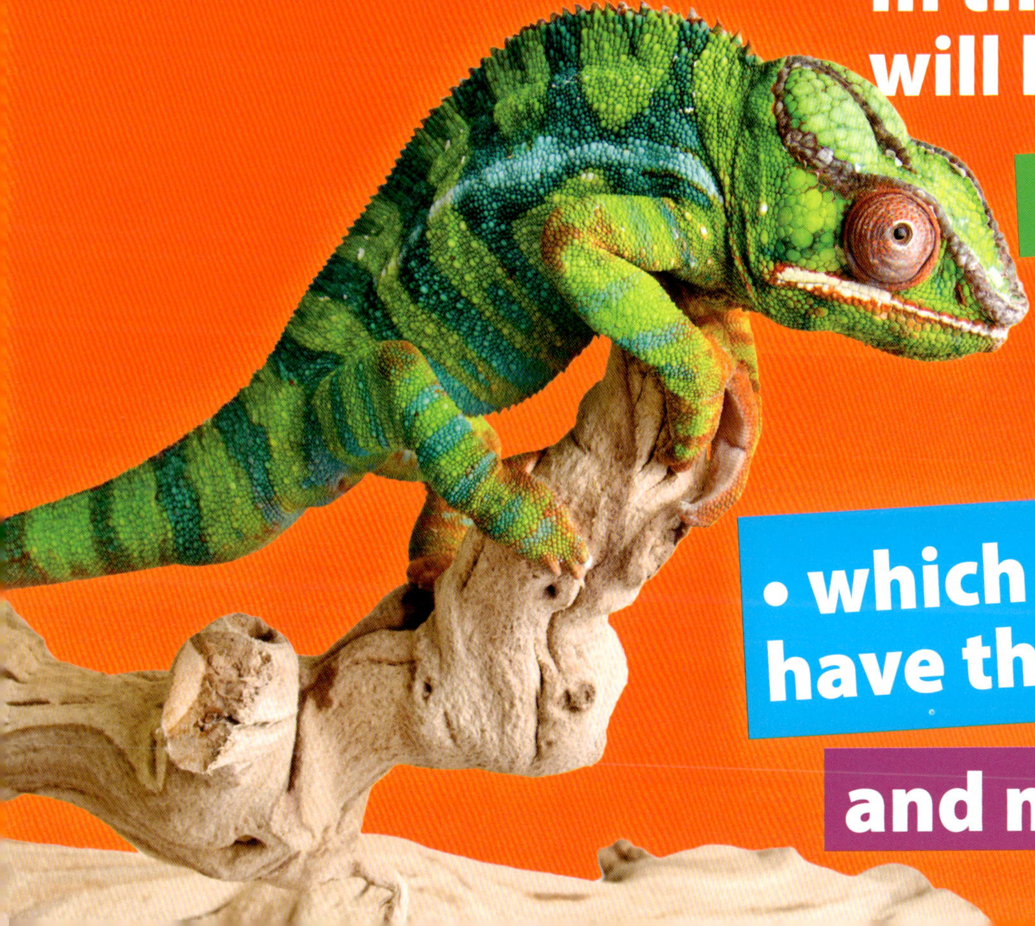

In this book, you will learn about

- what they are
- what they are for
- which animals have them

and much more!

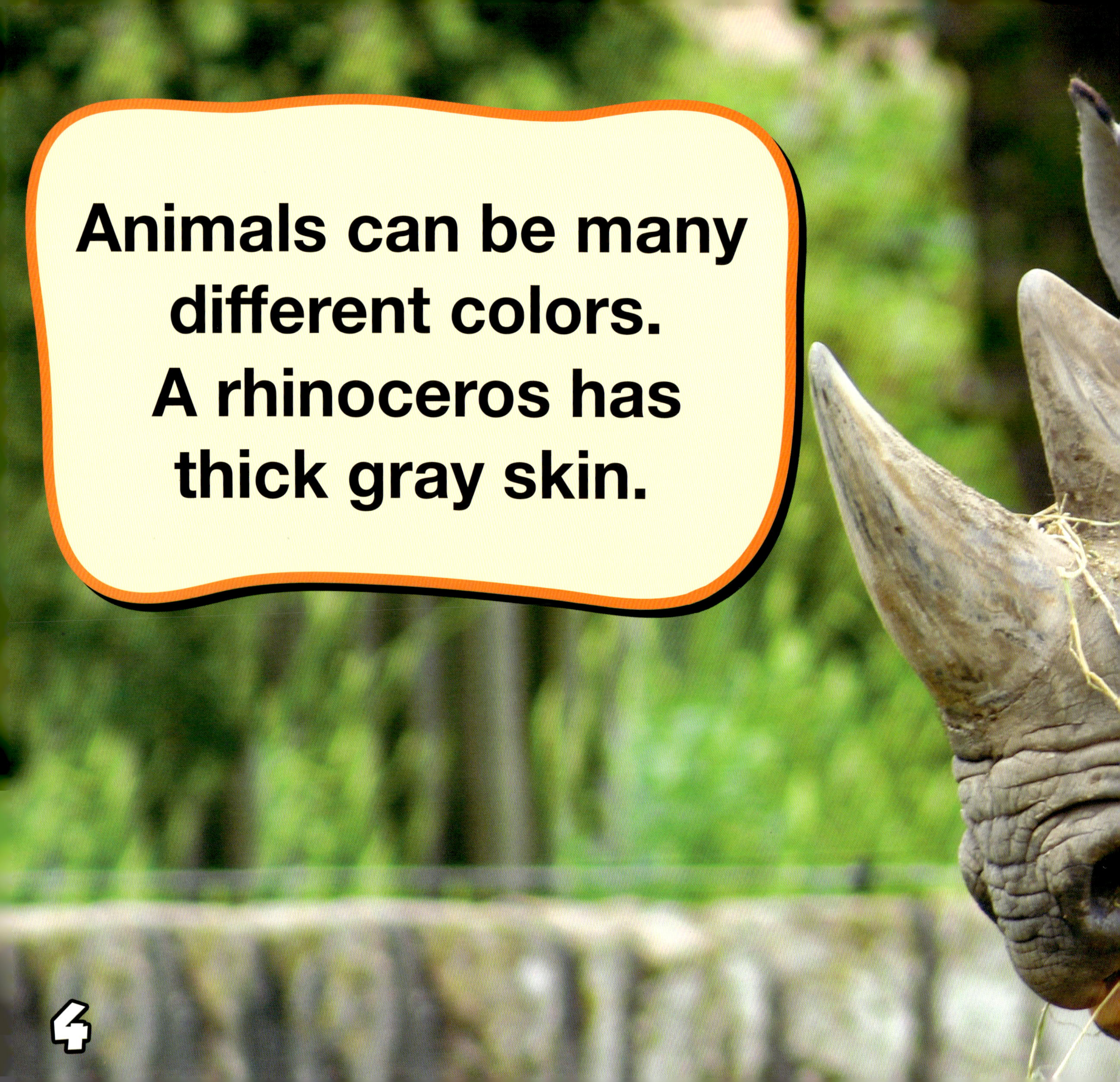

Animals can be many different colors. A rhinoceros has thick gray skin.

Some animals get their color from their fur. A mountain gorilla has black fur.

An orangutan has orange fur. Its fur covers almost all of its body.

One kind of animal can have different colors. Black bears can have black, gray, or brown fur.

Some birds have very colorful feathers. Peacock feathers are shiny blue and green.

A flamingo has pink feathers. The color comes from the small animals it eats.

Colors can help an animal stay safe. An iguana is green. This color helps it hide in plants.

A ladybug is red and black. Its bright color lets other animals know it tastes bad.

A lion has yellow fur. This helps it hide when it hunts in tall grass.

ANIMAL COLORS FACTS

Many **baby ducks** are **yellow**. They **change color** after about **six weeks**.

A **zebra** has **black** and **white** stripes. No zebras have the **same stripes**.

A **cuttlefish** can **change its** color to **hide** from other animals. This takes **less than a second**.

Tigers are orange with black stripes. They are the only cats with striped fur and skin.

There are 35 kinds of toucans. Different toucans come in many different colors.

A polar bear actually has clear fur. It looks white when light hits it.

KEY WORDS

Research has shown that as much as 65 percent of all written material published in English is made up of 300 words. These 300 words cannot be taught using pictures or learned by sounding them out. They must be recognized by sight. This book contains 36 common sight words to help young readers improve their reading fluency and comprehension. This book also teaches young readers several important content words, such as proper nouns. These words are paired with pictures to aid in learning and improve understanding.

Page	Sight Words First Appearance
4	a, animals, be, can, has, different, many
7	from, get, some, their
8	all, almost, an, is, its, of
11	have, kind, one, or
12	and, are, very
15	comes, eats, it, small
17	help, in, plants, this
18	know, lets, other
21	when

Page	Content Words First Appearance
4	colors, rhinoceros, skin
7	fur, mountain gorilla
8	body, orangutan
11	black bears
12	birds, feathers, peacock
15	flamingo
17	iguana
18	ladybug
21	grass, lion

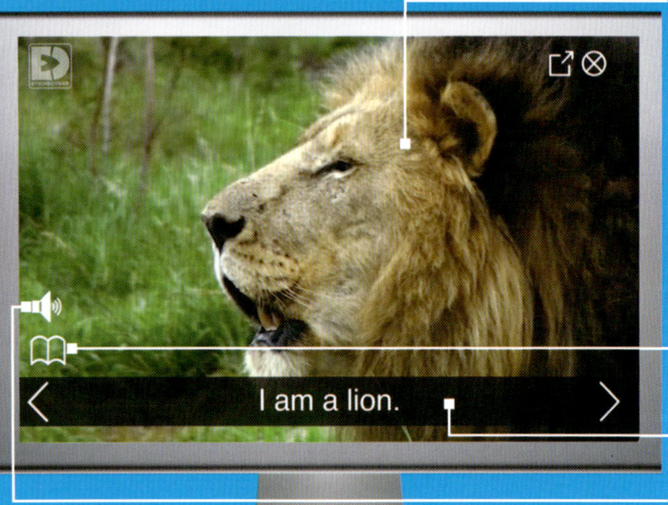

Watch
Video content brings each page to life.

Browse
Thumbnails make navigation simple.

Read
Follow along with text on the screen.

Listen
Hear each page read aloud.

Go to www.eyediscover.com and enter this book's unique code.

BOOK CODE

AVF25438